He Took
My Place

Jared Bellan

Scripture references taken from The Holy Bible, English Standard Version Copyright 2001 by Crossway Bibles, A publishing ministry of Good News Publishers, Wheaton, III

Webster's Dictionary Trident Reference Publishing, 2006 Montevideo, Mexico

Webster's Thesaurus Trident Reference Publishing, 2006

ISBN: 978-1-60383-285-4

Published by:
Holy Fire Publishing
717 Old Trolley Rd.
Atten: Suite 6, Publishing Unit #116
Summerville, SC 29485

www.ChristianPublish.com

Cover Design: Teresa Nicole

Printed in the United States of America and the United Kingdom

Dedication

This book is dedication first and foremost to the Glory of God. Furthermore, with much thankfulness and appreciation to all of you who have helped to raise me up as a Pastor. To my family, my precious wife Melissa, Brandon Watkiss, Ruth Fisher & team, Pastor Poole & Sharon Poole, the Pen-Del District of the Assemblies of God, and Benny Hinn Ministries. If you had not obeyed the Holy Spirit in joining in His process and plans for my life, I would not be where I am today. My prayer for all of you is that God will Bless you in many ways.

Many Thanks,

       Pastor Jared Bellan

Table Of Contents

Introduction

If you are looking for a closer walk with Christ, then "He Took My Place" will be a great tool that the Holy Spirit will use to take you closer to Jesus. Birthed out of the leading and outpouring of the Holy Spirit, "He Took My Place" is a book that explains the transformation of Jared Bellan and then teaches others how to walk in the supernatural power of God. A must read for all Christian's and spiritual leaders. Upon glancing at the title of the book, you may say "What does He Took My Place mean?" And so the book is an open invitation for you to open and read. This book covers everything that is necessary for a Christian including redemption, being led by the Spirit, healing & deliverance, and the foundations of the church. I pray that as you read this book that you enter with an open heart and a Bible in front of you so that the Lord may speak to you and so confirm in your heart the inspiration of this book. During this book at any time if you feel the presence of the Holy Spirit please put the book down and ask God what He is trying to speak to you. For the whole purpose of this book is to bring others into the transformational realm of walking in the redemption of Christ and the outpouring of the Holy Spirit. If you are not a Christian then let the Holy Spirit bring you to Christ through this transformational journey. But if you are a Christian then open your life to the Holy Spirit and let him fill you with the love of Christ so that you can be effective to touch the next generation. May God Bless you as you continue on this journey.

Pastor Jared Bellan

Chapter 1

Free Barabbas

Matthew 27:15-23 "Now at the feast the governor accustomed to release for the crowd any one prisoner whom they wanted. And they had then a notorious prisoner called Barabbas. So when they had gathered, Pilate said to them "Whom do you want me to release for you: Barabbas or Jesus who is called Christ?" For he knew that it was out of envy that they had delivered him up. Besides, while he was sitting on the judgment seat, his wife sent word to him, "Have nothing to do with that righteous man, for I have suffered much because of him today in a dream." Now the chief priest and the elders persuaded the crowd to ask for Barabbas and to destroy Jesus. The governor again said to them, "Which of the two do you want me to release for you?" And they said, "Barabbas." Pilate said to them, "Then what shall I do with Jesus who is called Christ?" They all said, "Let him be crucified!"

And he said, "Why, what evil has he done?" But they shouted all the more, "Let him be crucified!"

Let me borrow your life for about a minute. Well, let's say about fifteen minutes a day and take you on an exciting, dangerous, and event filled journey that will change your life. It happened over 2,000 years ago and still echoes through the walls of society today. It penetrates and shatters the earth with a thunderous quake. It is the evidence and nature of a holy transfer. A price that was paid that has changed reality itself. But let's first go to the story of Barabbas.

Barabbas the Criminal

Now Barabbas was a wicked man who lived a sinful lifestyle. Imagine the evil that follows such a man. He was an everyday criminal with a capital C. A criminal is someone who has committed an offense that violates a law. And a crime is a law that is broken. It is very important to remember this because it not only relates to our natural man, but also our supernatural.

Furthermore, this Barabbas lived a criminal's life. His life was filled with sin. He was motivated by evil thoughts that made people cringe when they saw him. There is Barabbas, they would say. He is a law-breaker, a criminal. He was not only a criminal, but a notorious one. That means that his sin made him popular. In this life, you are known by two things, your righteousness, meaning that which God has made righteous in your life, or your sin, meaning that which you have made evil in your life. Now Barabbas was known for his sin and it became so popular that it caused an uprising in the Roman Empire. And the Roman Empire was nobody to mess with.

Barabbas the Prisoner

Imagine all of a sudden evil stops in a life and justice is finally going to be brought to an offense that even other criminals are thankful when it is punished. I'm sure that is how others in the nation of Israel felt when Barabbas was arrested and sent to prison. The city and the Romans were thrilled that such a justice was brought and now some form of peace could be restored. Barabbas was chained and bound up to a prison cell.

Now prison cells in the Roman Empire were not American prison cells. They were much different and followed by torture. So this Barabbas fellow did not get his three meals a day as prisoners in the America would get. He did not get his exercise or recreation time. All that he would get is a beating, flogging, or some other kind of torture as he awaited his death sentence to be crucified.

I wonder the thoughts that went through the mind of Barabbas. Some may have been "I have finally been captured and now I am going to die for my wickedness." Others may have been "I don't care what you Romans say; I know that I am right." But whenever he laid his head down at night and it was silent, I am sure that he was afraid. Alone and frightened about what was going to happen. Would he finally face the consequence of his sin? Was it too late? Could he have done something that could have stopped this horrible situation from happening? The time drew closer and closer, until he suddenly fell asleep.

As soon as his eyes closed, there was a voice. Barabbas, get your filthy, nasty, no-good, self up and see what is going to happen with you. What is going to happen? Is it time for me to die?

A Savior's Life

Now let me take you to another place. A place called Nazareth. A town where people where known for their everyday labor and there poor conditions. This is the town where it was said "He shall be called a Nazarene." Can you fathom, that Jesus came out of this poverty stricken town. This Jesus was born some years ago in Bethlehem to a virgin named Mary. His earthly father was Joseph, but His real Father was Almighty God. He had brothers to play with, friends, and a real home. He was a kid, teenager, young adult, and man like anybody else. Well, almost. He was the Son of God. He lived in a human body, remembering all the Angels at His birth. Cherished all the promises of God and remembered the Father's purpose for Him. He worked an average job and was a carpenter by trade. Now a carpenter was a man who created wooden tables or chairs for people. He was a Creator by nature and a Creator in the flesh. Listen, Jesus was speaking to people by what He did. Many people knew that He was special and His special life was about to happen.

Prepare the Way

According to the Scriptures, it was sometime while Jesus was living His ordinary life as a man of God that somebody began preaching about the coming of the Messiah. This person was John the Baptist. Now John was far more than ordinary. He was a prophet and filled with the Holy Spirit from birth. The power of God was all over his life. He told the people to return to God with all their heart. He loved the sinner and rebuked the Pharisee. He was a true man of God. He was waiting for someone special. He was waiting for Jesus.

Suddenly, Jesus appeared to him and asked him to be baptized. John in his humbleness tried to refuse. But Jesus said that it must be done. Jesus was on His way to the cross. John 3:16 says "For God so loved the world that He gave His only begotten Son that whosoever believes in Him shall never die, but have eternal life."

Evidence of Christ

The evidence of Christ is seen in the power of Jesus Christ. The very first thing that Jesus did after entering into ministry was that He overcame Satan. The Spirit of God directed Jesus to go pray, fast, and overcome. It was that evidence of power that Satan was afraid of. He tried to manipulate Jesus in every way. Satan was afraid. You see, whenever there is an anointing, and an evidence of power, every demon shudders. Furthermore, when the spotless Son of God is there, then that means Satan is in trouble.

His First Stop

His first stop was Galilee. He went there to fulfill the Scripture "Land of Zebulun and land of Naphtali, the way to the sea, along the Jordan, Galilee of the Gentiles-" (Matthew 4:15). Fame began to spread about Him everywhere as He preached in the synagogues and healed the sick. If you remember, I said in the beginning of this book that you are remembered by either the good or the evil that you do in life. Jesus continued to do good by forgiving sins, healing those with physical problems, and delivering people from demons. He was ALL-Good and ALL-Powerful. He was the Son of God. He loved those who nobody else would love. He called people to follow Him from every walk of life. Jesus then proceeds to send them out in the power of the Holy

Spirit.

But one thing must happen. One thing that is even hard to imagine for the Son of God. He must die on the cross and take away the sins of the world. But there is only one problem. He has never felt the presence of Almighty God leave Him. And He will, once He goes to the cross.

His Journey

Suddenly, after a night of prayer, Jesus is arrested in the garden. He is taken. His disciples panic, one of them attacks a guard and cuts off his ear. But Jesus in all of His mercy still heals the sinner even when He is arrested for no reason. He goes with the officers and is now in arrest.

A Holy Transfer

According to the Scriptures, Isaiah prophesied that He was led like a lamb to the slaughter." Now you have to imagine, the Son of God was this lamb. He was willing to go in our place. It is amazing to me that Jesus went in our place. I call it a Holy Transfer. A transfer is when somebody gives you one thing in exchange for another. The only thing about this one is that it is HOLY. Holy means that something is perfect and set apart for a purpose. Jesus was this perfect Holy Transfer that would change the world forever.

Furthermore, Barabbas was in for a surprise and so are we, the Love of Jesus. He was at a point of destiny. For as soon as they said "Free Barabbas" he was freed.

You tell me, do you think that it is right for a murderer to go free? How about a terrorist or others who live a life of sin? HUH? I thought you would pause for a moment and not give an answer. The reason you did not give an answer is because in your heart your answer is NO. Hey, I understand. But you see Jesus love is different than ours. In Isaiah 55:8 the LORD says "For my thoughts are not your thoughts, neither are your ways my ways, declares the LORD."

He does not think like us nor does He need our approval about anything He does. He loves the sinner but hates the sin. He wants to let all in Heaven but can only let some. He does this because He is Holy and the only way to enter into Heaven is through Jesus.

Chapter 2

The Journey

Grab your suitcase. Get everything that you need. Your clothes, toiletries, and all other necessities for we are embarking on another journey. Well, to be honest it is similar to the first but a little bit more unpredictable. We are on a journey to the Living God. Webster's dictionary explains a journey in this way "the act of traveling or the distance traveled." So the act of traveling is a journey in itself. A walk of faith that takes you to places you never dreamed where possible. What an excitement. Let's get this journey moving.

The Act of traveling

So what does it mean to travel to God? What do you need to expect when embarking on a journey. If you would talk to the average missionary today he would probably tell you to "expect the unexpected and to enjoy every minute of it." Isn't that what we long for? To live a life of adventure! Have you ever gone on a roller coaster? I have to be honest, watching others ride is exciting to me, but to go on the ride is a journey. So then, we have the choice, to enjoy another's excitement or to have this excitement for ourselves. If you have never been on that roller coaster then you will never fully know what it would feel like to take the trip. My wife Melissa and I went on a journey for our honeymoon. We had a trip full of excitement that we have never taken before. It was full of questions as we discovered the sacredness and joy of marriage. We also swam with sting rays and sharks on our trip. I was scared stiff and so was my wife (And she did not know how to swim). But as soon as we entered the water something happened. The sting rays swam up to us and blew air on our feet. The instructor told us "they just gave you a kiss and a hug." And we were scared. Then it was off to the deep end and with much fear we swam with sharks. To be honest, I am a little overweight for my height and I thought here comes dinner. But just as we experienced joy with the sting rays, we also did with the sharks. I got so close to them that I could probably give them a hug. What a journey. You know the Scriptures talk to us about traveling. Mostly they talk to us about the act of traveling. Being prepared, counting the cost, and following instructions. Proverbs 16:9 says "In his heart a man plans his course, but the LORD determines his steps." So in this journey of life you may have planned your course and have your whole life figured out, but one encounter with the Living God will change it all. Are you ready? Do you have your spiritual bags packed? Then stop what you are doing right now! I want you to take five minutes to pray. Ask the Lord Jesus Christ to direct your steps this day. He will if you ask. But you better count the cost! You better know that you are not in control of your life anymore! Once Jesus forgives your sins and lives in your heart, you are not your own. By the way you never were. God created you for Him. He delights in you and He wants you. He wants you because He loves you. So what are you doing still listening to me? Go pray!

The Distance Traveled

So what did year hear? What did you feel? Was there a Holy tapping on your heart? Was there an excitement and joy? My prayers and hopes are that you hear the voice of God drawing you to this exciting journey. But let's take a moment to talk about the distance traveled. Jesus traveled the furthest distance to be able to reach you. In the lyrics of He came from Heaven to earth the songs says "He came from Heaven to earth to show the way, from the earth to the cross, my debt to pay, from the cross to the grave, from the grave to the sky, Lord I lift your name on high." Just think about it. The Son of God came down from Heaven to live in the body of a little baby. Now that is a journey. Think about the tenderness or dangers of being a baby. In our days babies can have many complications as they grow up. But in Jesus day it was much worse. Furthermore, for Him to humble Himself to this body of flesh is a journey that I believe nobody else was willing to take. He did this because He loves us so much that He was unwilling to let us go our own way. He made a perfect journey to an imperfect world so that the world would be changed forever.

Furthermore, Jesus was the first among many brothers. So He was the first to travel this journey of faith. Hold on Jared, what about the men and women of God in the Old Testament. Hey, I understand, but we are not in the Old Covenant any more. I love them, appreciate them, and hold the Old Testament as the Word of God as well, but you see we are in the New Covenant. That means that since Jesus was the first, we are the second. HUH? Jesus not only came to die for your sins but to make you into His image. He wants to restore, renew, fill and refill your life. He takes you from a sinner with a bag packed full of sin and un-packs the bag. Now your fleshly garbage is where it belongs, in the trash. And don't try to pick up garbage. It stinks. Grab your spiritual bag now and let Jesus fill it. For you are now a son and daughter of the Living God. Romans 9:25 says "As he said in Hosea: "I will call them "my people" who are not called my people; and I will call her "my loved one" who is not my loved one," and, "It will happen that in the very place where it was said to them, "You are not my people," they will be called "sons of the living God." Wow! Did you grasp that? You are second to Christ. If He is the Son and you are a son, then you are next in line as a child of God. That means that on this distance traveled that you can received anything Jesus received except for worship, praise, prayer and the throne of God. You can see Miracles, Signs, and Wonders. You can see lost humanity redeemed. A prisoner restored. A murderer set free. But on this journey, you need to make sure that you stay on course and finish the distance traveled.

Map

After going on a great expedition it is important to have a map. Have you ever tried to get somewhere and were unable to find it? Do you remember getting lost and turned around? You know today the biggest fad is a GPS. I have one on my telephone! It is great to be directed where to go and arrive at your destination in record time. But even with a worldly map you are subject to errors. But I have a map for you. One that will never get you lost. Listen to what the Word of God says about this map. 2nd Timothy 3:16 "All Scripture is God-breathed and is useful for teaching, rebuking, correcting, and training in righteousness, so that the man of God may be thoroughly equipped for every good work." Now that is what I'm talking about. A 100% proof map that can equip me to live a life that I was created to live. A life full of adventure!

My Journey

During my pre-teen and young adult life, I lived

a life of sin. I entered into an endeavor where my life was drifting from success to failure. Even though the recent years of my life were surrounded by drug dealing and drug abuse, I always found a way to cope with life. As a teenager, I constantly found myself in the back of police cars or having the police come to my parent's house. This was a constant reminder that my life was not on the right track.

From being raised in a very nice Catholic family, I found that I was on the opposite end of the ladder constantly addicted to drugs. While my father worked at a mill, my mother worked at the Beaver Falls Elementary School as a teacher's aide.

While attending Beaver Falls High School, I enjoyed playing football. This kept me busy and in shape as a young man. I played middle linebacker for the Beaver Falls Tigers were I was ranked 12th in the state.

Upon graduation from Beaver Falls High School, I searched different colleges trying to figure out what I was going to do. With living so close to the Community College of Beaver County (CCBC), it seemed that it would be a good decision to start attending college there. So I enrolled at CCBC for Criminal Justice. While attending school there, I figured that I could help other young kids who were in similar situations. After one semester, I enjoyed it and continued my studies there.

During this time, I was involved in a car accident on my way to school, and received a stress fracture in my spine due to the impact. This left me in a high level of pain where I was put on medication to relieve the symptoms. With these conditions, I was limited to what I could do. During this time, I struggled in school but was never the same since the car accident. But finally I finished school and graduated with my Associates Degree.

Because of the low income level in the Beaver County area, I transferred to Hawaii Pacific University located in downtown Honolulu, Hawaii. There I would pursue a Bachelor's Degree in Justice Administration. But due to failure in school I returned to the Beaver County area.

From this point on I started to drift down hill once again. Already taking medication for the pain in my back I started to be drink and do drugs. When this happened, I began to revert to my old ways of living. On top of all of this, I was going to have a son.

But late in the fall, I was arrested near Geneva College and God was bringing my old lifestyle to an end. While spending thirty days in jail I was being drawn to the only One who could help, the One who called Himself the way, the truth and the life. It led me to a church service where for the first time in my life everything made sense. I started to realize that without Jesus in my life there was no hope for me at all. So I accepted Jesus Christ as my personal savior. Shortly after a preacher named Reverend Tench came to visit me. We talked about all kinds of things. I told him my decision to accept Christ and he smiled. But in the middle of the conversation he told me that maybe one day I would be a great preacher. I did not pay much attention to him at the time but God reminded me of it later.

I cried out to the Lord to please heal my back and take care of my son that would soon be born. Jesus healed me and set me free from my sin. My mother decided to post bond for me after I was there for 30 days.

After all of this, I began to talk to Pastor Watkiss at First Assembly of God in Beaver Falls, Pa. We became good friends but I still had a problem. My son was soon to be born and I was going to be sentenced for my crime.

On November 23, 2004, my son Jayden was born. Jayden was transferred to West Penn due to complications and would undergo treatment. My family and I drove down to see him. With tubes in his mouth and barely breathing, I could only ask God to please show me a sign that he was going to be alright.

Whenever I touched his hand, he held on, and before long he opened his eyes for the first time.

In the meantime, I was going for my sentencing where I would receive 16 months of probation which was a miracle in itself. God began to do many miracles things in my life. He gave me favor everywhere I went and His blessing always followed.

God also started speaking to my heart calling me to ministry. I prayed and asked God if He was sure. In the middle of my prayer the mail man came to the door and dropped off the mail. I would never interrupt my prayers but something told me to pursue it. So I did. It was a paper from Christian Urban Biblical Ministry and Geneva College asking me if I was interested in pursuing a full time ministry major. So I pursued the call of God. With no money for school I believed that if God wanted this He would provide. By the beginning of August God had provided above and beyond what I had expected. I ended up receiving free schooling with $2,000-3,000 dollars left over. After completing eight months of probation God provided to pay off my fine and I was finished with probation.

During this time I was baptized in water and the Holy Spirit with the initial physical evidence of speaking in tongues. This brought me into a deeper relationship with God and soon after I began to see miracles, signs and wonders in my ministry. I began working with Ruth Fisher who took over the Kathryn Kuhlman ministry.

Furthermore, during this time I experienced a great move of the Spirit where I met my wife Melissa. We fell in love and God confirmed in our hearts that we needed to get married. After we were married Melissa adopted Jayden and became his mother. This is one of the greatest miracles that I witnessed in my life. And there are many other things to share with you that God has done in my life. But we will talk about them later on in this book.

As of now, I am serving the Lord, a great husband, Father, living free from sin, addiction, and preaching & teaching others how to serve the Lord Jesus Christ. My prayer for you is that as you read on, the Holy Spirit will reveal Jesus to you in a special way.

Chapter 3

He Takes Away Sins

So what is a sin? In the previous chapters, I talked with you about Jesus Christ. About a journey and an excursion that is worth dying for. Now I want to talk to you about sin. If I do not talk to you about this whole matter, you could possibly continue to do something that could be detrimental to your journey. Sin is a dark barrier reef. A black hole that tries to bring death to everything it touches. And before we go any further, we will talk about this issue.

Origin of Sin

Now whenever we talk about the origin of sin, we have to go to its roots. Sin's roots are found in one person. Satan. He is the author of sin. In Isaiah 14:12 the Word of God says "How you have fallen from heaven, O morning star, son of the dawn! You have been cast down to the earth, you who once laid low the nations! You said in your heart, "I will ascend to heaven; I will raise my throne above the stars of God; I will sit enthroned on the mount of the assembly, on the utmost heights of the sacred mountains. I will ascend above the tops of the clouds; I will make myself like the Most High."

The origin of sin is found in Satan trying to be God or to be a god. Jesus also has much to say about this in Luke 10:18- "He replied, "I saw Satan fall like lightning from heaven." Furthermore, since he fell from Heaven, he is fallen & sinful. His nature is to ensnare. He brings destruction to lives and destroys families. He does this through one thing, sin.

Sin is like a magnet. It has a force behind it that attracts people just the same way that an ordinary magnet attracts metal. Whenever the object of its choice is close enough, it goes for its prey. We call this temptation. It leaves you confused, angry, upset, and if followed can destroy your life.

21st Century Sins

Now let's talk about today! You know the only difference between today and the centuries before is technology. But sin has always been sin. It takes different forms and sometimes we feel like if we do not see that specific sin in the Bible, then it is ok to do. So I want to give you a 21st Century Holy Ghost chat. And I pray that as we do, you do not place my book in the garbage.

The first venues of sins are found in the Bible. Some of them are disobeying God's voice, not obeying the Word of God, murder, rape, stealing, incest, and etc. But the sins we will discuss in detail are found in Galatians 5. The Bible says these sins are sexual immorality, impurity, debauchery, idolatry, witchcraft, jealousy, selfish ambition, dissensions, factions, envy, drunkenness, and orgies.

Sexual immorality is sexual intercourse outside of marriage. This also relates to homosexuality that is found in 1 Corinthians 6:9 and 1 Timothy 1:10.

Furthermore, this applies to pornography. The word pornography comes from the root word porneia. This means to take pleasure in viewing pictures, films, writings, or anything else that relates to viewing a women or a male that is naked. (Ex 20:14; Matthew 5:31-32; 19:9; Acts 15:20,29, 21:25; 1 Cor 5:1)

Impurity is considered as sexual sins, evil deeds and vices. This also includes thoughts and desires of the heart. (Eph 5:3; Col 3:5) This relates to the heart and the mind of a man or women. Jesus said as a man thinks so also he does. And out of the abundance of the heart the mouth speaks. So the sin of impurity is a sin that occurs out of the wicked desires of the heart or mind.

Debauchery is the sin of sensuality. This means to follow one's own desires and passions to the point of having no shame or public decency. (2nd Cor 12:21) The sin of debauchery can be closely related to prostitution and public exposure of one's own sin. This can also relate to a criminal, gang member, or terrorist.

Idolatry is the worship of spirits, persons, graven images, and trust in any person, institution or thing as having equality or oneness with God or His Word. (Col 3:5) You see the sin of idolatry is a selfish sin and is commonly related to other religions. Since the LORD is the only God and is represented in three distinct persons, the Father, the Son, and the Holy Spirit, then all other references and religions, texts, or manuscripts other than the Bible is the sin of idolatry. Some of these religions include Islam, Buddhism, mysticism, psychics, mediums (consulting the dead), Satanist, church of scientology, Mormon, Jehovah's Witness, witchcraft, and anything else that sets itself up to be God or have final authority.

Witchcraft is the sin of spiritism, sorcery, black magic, worship of demons and the use of drugs to produce spiritual experiences. (Ex 7:11, 22, 8:18, Rev 9:21; 18:23) The sin is common among those who live in black market and street environment. Witchcraft is also seen in rising music performers and entertainers.

Discord is the sin of quarreling, antagonism; and the struggle for superiority. (Rom 1:29; 1 Cor 1:11; 3:3) To be exact, this is a sin that is predominately found in the life of unbelievers and can be found in some believers. This is commonly seen in churches were people in the church disrespect leadership and authority. It can also be seen in a criminal's life and the lack of submission to the government, rulers, and authorities.

Jealousy is resentfulness or envy of someone else or their possessions. (Ro 13:13, 1 Cor 3:3) This can happen whenever somebody is not happy or joyful with what God has provided or with what they have. And through temptation they fall into sin, strive to be better, and obtain what the person that they are jealous of has.

Selfish ambition is the unrighteous decision to seek power of a position in order to rule or lord it over someone. (2nd Cor 12:20; Php 1:16-17) This can happen when an individual is thriving to control everyone and everything. He or she then takes it into action. This is called selfish ambition.

Dissensions are the introduction of divisive teachings that are not in accordance or supported by God's Word. (Ro 16:17) This can include the every rising and craze of the feel good gospel. A gospel that is full of materialism. Jesus does love and does have blessings for His people, but it is in accordance with serving Him and obeying His Word.

A faction is the sin of divisions in the congregation or groups of people that form cliques that destroy unity in the church. (1 Cor 11:9) This can also relate to outside the church and can be compared to the divisions of people, organizations, and authorities. When this sin occurs, authentic relationships can never form because of distrust.

Envy is the sin of being resentful or disliking a person who has something that one desires. This can happen through ones heart and desire to hate someone.

Once this occurs it always leads to separation from the individual.

Drunkenness is impairing ones mental or physical state by an alcoholic drink. This sin is predominant throughout the world and is not accepted by Christ. And since the current government statistics are that one drink impairs someone's judgment, then it can be easily said that all drinking of alcohol is a sin.

An orgy is the excessive feasting and revelry; a party spirit involving alcohol, drugs, sex, or the like. This sin is commonly seen in college students and in criminal or gang environments. This sin leads to the destruction of one's life and can destroy one's ability or mental state.

Furthermore, as it relates to the 21st Century, there are some sin's that are not listed in the Word of God that we will talk about. Some of these are cigarettes, drugs, and suicide. These sins are not accepted by Christ and can cause you to be separated from Christ. The Apostle Paul goes on to clearly state that those who practice these sins whether a believer or unbeliever, shut themselves out from the Kingdom of God, and they do not possess eternal salvation. (Gal 5:21; 1 Cor 6:9)

Consequence of Sin

Ok, now that the Holy Spirit has dealt with you about sin and has shown you the origin of it, let's talk about why you should not do it! Have you ever heard that you reap what you sow? Well there is an ancient principle that was founded when the world was created. It's called sowing and reaping. You can either sow good seed and receive a good harvest or sow sin and receive a sinful harvest. But there is a big difference. The good seed is sown into righteousness and the sinful seed is sown into unrighteousness. One leads to life and one leads to death. Both can create results in Heaven and on Earth. The righteous seed can create good results in your life while the other can create results that separate you from Heaven and bring destruction to your life on earth. The one seed affects the other. But it is your choice. You have the seed. It's your earthly temple. You were made in the image of God and so you have a seed. God's image! But I want to talk to you now about the consequence of the sinful seed and the results of that seed.

In Genesis 3, we have an encounter with the sinful seed. It is the first account that a human being chooses to sow it. It is Adam and Eve. Most of you already know this story or have heard it since you were a kid. But listen, this is important to your life. If you miss this, you will miss everything. The serpent deceived Adam and Eve by tempting them with the sinful seed. They took it and saw in immediate result. Oh the knowledge of God they must of thought. Oh the great reward of the seed. But there was a problem. The LORD was about to confront them and the serpent. The Bible says that the LORD came walking in the garden and was calling for the man. God is calling for you too! Hello, where are you? What is this you have done? Why have you done it? God deals with Adam and Eve about their sin. There is a sinful harvest. A separation from God, a curse on man to work hard physical labor and only reap by the sweat of his brow, the womb of the women cursed and pain will come upon her at birth, and the serpent was ultimately cursed. If you throw a stone on the water there is a ripple. This ripple causes other ripples behind the first. That is how sin works. You may not see all of its effects, but one day you will when you stand before the throne of Almighty God. Adam and Eve knew that if they ate the fruit it was sin. Understand this, you know what sin is. And don't give me the garbage that everything will be ok and Jesus still loves me. Surely He still loves you, but all your sin must be washed away under His blood. All your sin must be repented of. Listen; stop listening to your flesh. All through the Bible men and women would not repent. Calamity would always occur in their lives. If you do not heed the conviction of the Holy Ghost, calamity will fall

45

upon you and your household.

So listen closely to me. If you live a life of sin, you will first be spiritually separated from God. You will not feel His Presence. Then you will reap your sinful harvest and suffer greatly. Then you will be eternally separated from God and be sent to Hell when you leave the earth. But you do have a choice. And when you stand before God, it is too late. Either you lived for Christ or you didn't. It's that simple.

My Sin

I knew I figured you out preacher. I knew I got you. You lived just the same way I lived. Yes, I did. I used to live that way is the answer. Remember, I lived an ungodly lifestyle before I came to Christ and through deciding to live a sinful lifestyle I reaped the most horrible things in my life. Listen, I am being serious. Sin hurts! It destroys! It kills!

The first thing that I want to talk to you about is the destruction to my family. As I said, I have a very nice family. But I destroyed them and broke relationships with them that I had built for years. I was seen as a troubled child. My mother wept bitterly as she would wait sometimes by the telephone to hear whether I was coming home or not. What an experience to put someone through. How ignorant of me to punish someone that loved me. It took years of grace and restoration from God to bring us where we are today.

The next thing is my life. I was a bright young man and had many things going for me. But I chose to fill my flesh with sin. I chose to sow a sinful seed and reap sinful results.

The last thing is my image. I chose to associate myself with sin. Everybody who knew me understood that I was a trouble maker. This destroyed my image in the community. But ultimately, it destroyed God's image.

He Takes Away Sins

By now you are probably tired of hearing about

sin and are probably feeling pretty horrible about the decisions that you have made in your life. But listen friend, there is hope. The Bible says that He appeared to take away sins. So then, there is hope for the sinner and the broken. If you have ever been there or struggled with sin then get ready for a mighty cleansing stream of blood that is coming your way. It is the blood of Jesus.

For there is a promise from God that says He wants to reason with you today. Isaiah 1:18 says "Come now, Let us reason together, says the LORD. "Though your sins are like scarlet, they shall be as white as snow, though they are red as crimson, they shall be like wool. If you are willing and obedient, you will eat the best from the land; but if you resist and rebel, you will be devoured by the sword." For the mouth of the LORD has spoken."

Praise the LORD! Did you hear that correctly? Almighty God wants to reason with you. Now I want you to understand what it means to reason. Webster's dictionary says that the word reason means to explain an action or a cause to believe. O' listen to me friend, God is giving you a reason to believe. The reason is the washing of your sins. Just look at your life. The choices you make. The thoughts you think. The LORD is saying to you come here and let's talk. Can you imagine? And you thought that God was always pointing the finger at you saying no, no, no. You got it wrong friend. God is saying yes, yes, yes. Come over here where the cleansing stream is. Where the blood of Jesus Christ is! Where there is blessing and where nothing that is fashioned against you shall prosper. It is the place of the good seed. So I want to give you the choice right now to have the good seed placed in you. The Bible says that we have an imperishable seed in us that is if Christ is in you. So I want you to make a decision to have this imperishable Christ in you. If you are sincere and want Jesus Christ in your life please agree with me in prayer. Dear Jesus, I believe that you died in my place, I believe that you are the Son of God,

I ask that you take my sins and forgive them, I believe that Almighty God raised You from the dead and I ask that you would come into my heart. I now confess you as Lord and Savior of my life in Jesus Name, Amen. I want you to begin confessing Jesus as your Lord and Savior. All those sins are gone. It is finished. All of your past is gone. Praise God!

Our Righteousness

Okay, I see your point Jared. I have just given my heart to Christ or I have just repented of my sin. How do I live this Christian life? Isn't that all of our questions. It sounds good when we read it or when the preacher preaches it. But when it comes down to it, do you fail to obey Christ?

I have an answer to your question. Jesus Christ is your righteousness. So stop trying to form your own. Romans 10:4-11 says "Christ is the end of the law so that there may be righteousness for everyone who believes. Moses describes in this way the righteousness that is by the law: "The man who does these things will live by them." But the righteousness that is by faith says: "Do not say in your heart, 'Who will ascend into heaven? (That is, to bring Christ down) "Or 'Who will descend into the deep?" (That is to bring Christ up from the dead). But what does it say? The word is near you; it is in your mouth and in your heart," that is, the word of faith we are proclaiming: That if you confess with your mouth, "Jesus is Lord," and believe in your heart that God raised him from the dead, you will be saved. For it is with your heart that you believe and are justified, and it is with your mouth that you confess and our saved. As the Scripture says, "Anyone who trust in him will never be put to shame."

For lift up your eyes unto the hills, where does your help come from, it comes from the LORD the maker of Heaven and Earth. He who keeps you will not slumber, ye He who keeps you will not sleep. For the LORD neither sleeps nor slumbers or grows tired or weary. For He who watches over you is able to guide you into all truth. He is your LORD and your God this day. So when He calls for you, when His Spirit fills you, when He says come away My Beloved, listen to Him. He will keep you obedient to His Word. He says that nobody can snatch you from the Father's hand. He will not leave you as an orphan, because you have a Father. But you have to listen to His voice, His Spirit, and His Word. The same way that you accepted Jesus in your heart is the same way you live your Christian life. You never expected to be a Christian did you? Or did you wake up one day and say that is it "I will be a Christian!" No you didn't, the Spirit of God moved upon your life. So let Him continue to move. Don't be rebellious or there will be no fruit in your life. That is why you have witnessed other people who called themselves Christian, but do not act or live like one. They have decided to run from that moving of the Spirit in their life. It is not the church. It is them. But you do not have to be like them. You can and will be led by the Spirit of God if you let Christ mold your life.

Chapter 4

He Takes Away Pain

So far you have come through almost half of the book, received much grace, and are continuing to understand the depths of the love of God. But now, we will be talking about a matter that is near and dear to God's heart. It's called Healing. Healing is the physical proof of the existence of God and His care for those who suffer with pain. Webster says that "pain is a disagreeable sensation caused by injury or severe suffering." And disease or illness is always a result of that suffering.

Pain is Temporary

I think one of the greatest things we can understand when dealing with physical pain is that it is temporary. The Bible says that there is a time and season for everything under Heaven. There is a time when we will have pain and a time when we will not.

So we can find great comfort that His mercies are new each day.

So how was your day today? Was it good, bad, or horrible? I bet one thing about your day is that it was different. Things happened today that did not happen yesterday. Your body maybe felt better today than yesterday. Your job could have been better or worse, or your family life could be better or worse. Isn't that remarkable! Each day was different, exciting, and new. But it was temporary.

You know life in itself is a great joy. We go through things and end up places that we would have never dreamed were possible. But sometimes along the road, even those things will come to an end. And so it is with pain. Your pain or disease will someday come to an end.

So you go to the doctors and find out that something horrible has happened to your body. Or you get a test done at the hospital and find that you have a major illness like cancer, heart disease, or diabetes. Next you're in line at the pharmacy getting pills to help your temporary condition.

You see, a prescription is a temporary answer to a permanent problem. The temporary problem is "your pain" and the temporary solution is "your prescription." But there is no hope in that. I am not telling you to stop taking your prescriptions, but what I am telling you to do is to find a permanent solution to your temporary problem. Most of the time a person's permanent solution is surgery. Hey, I'm not against surgery either. I love doctors and believe that God has placed them here to help. But they are human. Understand that! They can only see things from an earthly perspective because that is how they are trained. However, some doctors are Christians and I am very thankful for all of you because you have more to offer than the world does. But listen, even Christian doctors cannot fully solve your problems because God has already chosen a source of healing that is permanent. But the key to being healed is not going to the next greatest crusade or meeting, (and not that meetings or crusades are bad, I have Healing meetings of my own) but to the source of healing. And when approaching this source, we must let Him into our temporary problems.

Permanent Solution

I believe the number one reason people do not get healed is because they fail to let Jesus into their temporary problems. They cry O' LORD heal me, touch me, help me, and cleanse me. But they do not let Him in. The Word of God says "Be still and know that I am God." You must be still after worshipping Him, reading the Word, and then let Him in. Too many Christians miss this. That is why so many non-believers get healed. They go to a Miracle Service and sing a couple songs, hear the Word of God, release their faith, and then they LET HIM IN. Listen, they are just open and know that nothing else has done it or can do it. So if it works, it's worth a try. And so they are healed. You tell me, when you let a doctor perform an operation, you let him in to your flesh to try and help you right? Absolutely! How else would you get help? So it is the same way with healing. You have to let Him be permanently present in every situation. Furthermore, since pain is an act of suffering, then pain can be more than physical. But the Bible says in Isaiah 53 that he bore our grief and carried our sorrows. That He was pierced for our transgressions and by His stripes we are healed. He already made the way. Before Jesus went to the cross, He was scourged. That meant they took pieces of metal to His flesh. They crushed Him physically. That is where your healing comes from. The cross was an offering of the perfect Son of God to forgive sins, but the wounds of Christ were for your healing. Jesus is your permanent solution.

Furthermore, today God is present on earth through the person of the Holy Spirit. Remember the Father, Son, and Holy Spirit. It is the Holy Spirit who is present on earth to make the wounds and blood of Christ a reality to the world.

I don't know about you but the Holy Spirit's power is far greater than any other force on earth. He is the one who holds the world together. He is stronger than all of the nuclear weapons put together and if He left the world, it would fall apart.

He holds the world together and His power operates through faith in Jesus Christ. If you put your faith in Christ one day your healing will come. Your physical body is a body that God is interested in. He made it in His image and He wants to restore His image.

My Healing

As I said before, there were many things in my life that led me to a total surrender to the love of Christ. One of those things is healing. Healing is an act of unmerited grace that changes our perspective on Christ. He is so real! He is present in this place! He is here! These are some of those things that I realized when God healed me.

My healing happened as I cried out to God for mercy. I suffered a horrible stress fracture in my spine plus a condition call spondalosdysis. That means my back was "slightly broken" and one of my hip & lower back bones were higher than the other ones. I went to almost every doctor in Beaver County, Pennsylvania trying to get some relief. But all that the doctors would offer were pills, pills, and more pills. Some of them had me go for treatments like shoving a needle in my neck and spine. Others had me get acupuncture treatments, shot electric currents through my body, and put me on medicine that they gave to cancer patients. It was horrible. So I struggled with this condition until I experienced my healing.

It happened one night after I gave my life to Christ. I was depressed, frustrated, and tired of the pain. The only thing I had to take was Tylenol. Anyone who has pain as I did knows that Tylenol does absolutely nothing. I cried, wept, and pleaded with God. Please heal me Lord, I said. I know that if you don't heal me I am going to go back to the doctors because of this pain and end up on pain pills. Lord, you know me. I will end up living the same kind of life I used to. Please heal me Lord. I'm sorry about all of these horrible things I have done. Please Lord. Then I went to sleep.

The next day I woke up pain free. Praise the LORD. I can remember walking and all that kept going through my mind is by His stripes we are healed. The funny thing is that I was not too familiar with the Bible to know many of those verses. God was birthing in my heart a ministry and an anointing for the sick.

Furthermore, my son Jayden was going to be born addicted to drugs and it was later on that God healed him. I can remember it well. My family and I went to West Penn hospital to see Jayden. His eyes were closed and his body red like he was in a fire. The nurse told me that she has done all that she could do. He was not opening his eyes and was not taking fluids properly. I remember opening up the incubator where tubes were placed all through his body. In my heart I said Lord, please have mercy on him. Please heal him just like you touched me and changed me. Then I blew on his belly and grabbed his finger. Jayden suddenly grabbed my finger and opened his eyes for the first time. Praise the LORD! The nurses were amazed and the doctors said that he was a miracle baby. Jayden was healed and we have a doctor confirmed report that he is a normal child. Today Jayden is a little 4 year old bundle of joy to everyone in our family. He enjoys the beach, playing with trains, and going to church. He loves the Lord and knows were his healing came from. One day I asked him if he remembered about the hospital and he told me yes. He said that he felt the Lord there with him and one of his first words was Jesus. I believe that Jesus was Jayden's permanent solution. How about you? What is your permanent solution? What is the first thing you do when faced with pain or trouble? Do you run to a temporary solution? Or do you go to a permanent one?

Healing in the 21st Century

So, are there healings that happen today? That is one question you might ask? My church told me there is no more healing other than spiritual! Or that is great for you but what about my healing? Does it come in the same way?

My answer to your question is that God is the great miracle worker. He can do any miracle any time He wants. But it will always be fresh and new. But it happens through faith in Jesus Christ. It happens when the gospel is preached. You know the life, death, and resurrection of Christ.

So why did I not get healed yet Jared? I hear the gospel all the time! Stop listening to the devil! You just have never applied the gospel to your whole man. You just applied it to eternity. So you got an eternal reward. But the gospel is a whole gospel. It means that He has saved all and has been made LORD of all.

As a minister of the gospel, I have seen many eyewitness accounts of healings. And since I do not have 500 pages to write all of them, I will give you some of them. Many of them happened while I ministered with Ruth Fisher in her healing meetings at South Hills Assembly of God in Bethel Park, PA. The others have happened across America as I preached the gospel with my wife Melissa, and others have happened while I was ministering with Ruth Fisher at a Benny Hinn Miracle Service in Hershey, Pa & Pittsburgh, Pa.

As I look back at all of these healings that have taken place, I see the love of Christ. There was a woman who came to us who had not walked for 10 years. Her daughter brought her seeking help. So we prayed for her and she began to walk. Praise the LORD! Another was a woman with a tumor on her head. Her sister had come to the meeting that night asking for prayer for her sister. I was impressed by the Lord to pray for the sick women's sister. I then told her to go to her sister and lay hands on her immediately. So as she was preparing to do this after she left, she saw that her sister had come to the meeting. She laid hands on her and the next day a miracle was confirmed by surgeons. They went to do the surgery and as they were trying to find the tumor to remove it, it was gone. They asked her if she had surgery somewhere else. She said no, and rejoiced for God had healed her.

Another healing is of a woman from Industry. Her name is Patti. She is a close friend of mine and was healed of a nerve disorder. She suffered greatly with pain for many years. This affected her life, family, and walk with the Lord. Before her healing, she was a Catholic and very dedicated to the Lord.

She heard about one of the healing services that we were holding at Greater Faith Family Worship Center in Industry, Pa. It was a miracle itself that she even knew of the meeting. You see, we do very little advertisement. The majority of it is word of mouth. She found out about the meeting on the internet. Her son was in Chicago and knew the pain that his mother was going through. So he began looking for healing services in that area. He came across First Assembly of God's website and somehow found my itinerary. She arrived at the service and was one of the many who were physically healed. Today, she is a blessing to the LORD. She now attends a Christian church and is going to be used by God in a mighty way.

The last touch of the Holy Ghost that I want to talk about is the deliverance from demonic possession & oppression. A person who is attacked by a demon suffers much pain in every area of their life.

We were at South Hills Assembly of God for our annual monthly Miracle Service. During the offering time a women jumped out of the aisles and yelled "please help sir?" I asked her what was wrong. She told me that this man next to her was suffering from demonic oppression and demonic dreams. So I assured her that after the offering, I would talk to Ruth and we would pray for her. As I walk down to the front of the sanctuary, the LORD spoke to me. He said "There is more." There are others that are suffering from demonic oppression. So I told the people that there are many here tonight who are suffering from demonic oppression. You have demonic dreams and attacks. God wants to set you free. I wish you were there. It was the most beautiful sight as 15-20 young adults jumped over seats and ran to the front. As soon as they got there I said "Spirit of Unrest" I command you to leave in the name of Jesus. This demonic spirit is found in Psalm 91 and is a result of not drawing near to God in prayer. But this night God was giving grace. As soon as the word was given the people began to tremble and shake as the power of God shook that foul demon off of every area of their life. Many of them came back next month to tell us the good news that all the attacks have stopped. One woman was a nurse and because of these demonic dreams she could not study to pass her nursing exams. She was set free, passed her nursing exams with one of the top percentages, and she brought her first patient to the LORD. How about that! That is why I obey God. To touch a life and see God make something out of nothing.

Furthermore, time does not permit me to tell more. The cancers, tumors, HIV, STDS, legs, backs, knees, blind eyes, feet, pain, deliverance from demonic oppression, and drug abuse. God is good. He loves you even when you don't love yourself. He loved you even when you didn't love Him & before the world was even created.

So what about your pain? Are you willing to let the "LORD OUR HEALER" Heal you? I want to pray a simple prayer with you. Father, you know our hearts and you know our pain, I pray for whoever is reading this book that you inspired me to write. Lord, I ask that you heal them of every disease or pain that they have. And I rebuke pain, sickness, and disease in the name of Jesus Christ. Now stand up and move that part of your body that you have pain with or do something that you could not do before. For God loves you and is able to heal all your diseases.

Chapter 5

He Took My Place

All the world stops to see, listen, and hear the grace that has been poured out. Can you imagine? A love so pure, so rich, so strong that reaches far above the heaven's. That is the love of Christ that we are talking about. It is richer than honey and finer than gold. 1 Corinthians 13:4-8 says "Love is patient, love is kind. It does not envy, it does not boast, it is not proud. It is not rude, it is not self seeking, it is not easily angered, it keeps no record of wrongs. Love does not delight in evil but rejoices with the truth. It always protects, always trust, always hopes, always perseveres. Love never fails. That is the kind of love we need. The kind that never fails!

Patient Love

God is patient with you friend. He saw you while you lived in sin. He patiently waited for you to hear the message of Christ. When you heard the Word of Truth you wrestled with it in your flesh, but He still waited and tugged at your heart. He knows everything that you go through and is so patient that He continues to convict you of sin your entire life until you give your life to Christ or take your last breath.

Kind Love

His love is kind towards you. It was Jesus who took your place. Think about how kind His love is that He would spend many years in the body of an infant awaiting to die for you. I don't know about you, but that is kind. Infants are gentle, soft, cuddly, and very loving.

Furthermore, the love of a child is like no other kind of human love. I cherish when Jayden tells me that he loves me. Furthermore, I can imagine Mary & Joseph's reaction when baby Jesus hugged them and said "I love you." What a kind love. You know, He feels the same way about you. Jesus is reaching out to you and saying "Come, let me wrap my loving presence around you." O' the comfort and peace that He can give! O' His kindness! If you are in a place in your life where you need kindness, feel free to reach out your hands and say Father; please let me feel your kindness. I can guarantee that He will show you His kindness in many different ways.

Love that never fails

I love this part of God's love. His love can never fail me. While I may fail Him at times and make mistakes. His love will never fail me.

I remember several times as a new Christian where every time there was an altar call I would go up. I knew that His love would never fail me and today I still recognize that His love is what holds me together. I rest with that conviction everywhere I go. While love between close family and friends will fail at times, I know that His love will never fail me. Every time I think that I am far away from His love, He reminds me in tangible ways that He is there. Jesus surely did take my place on that cross. He took my place in that prison cell. I should have died in my sin and went to Hell. I should have suffered with my pain. I should have remained on drugs. But God's love was greater. He knew my condition. My sinfulness! He knows the beginning to the end. It excites me when I think about His great love. When times get tough! When days feel like they will never end! I thank Him for His love!

So what about your life? Are you doubtful of His love? Do you have those tough days? I still do at times. But one thing is that you can put all you have on His love and rest in assurance that it is far greater than life itself.

Chapter 6

Sovereign Mercy

I want to talk to you about something the Holy Spirit has been burning into my heart. So if you are longing to hear "Thus Saith the LORD" then you better get ready for a powerful, life changing Word straight from the throne of Almighty God. The Word is called Sovereign Mercy.

First let's turn to the Word of God in the ninth chapter of Romans. Here we find a powerful Word that will change your life forever. Romans 9:1-33 "I am speaking the truth in Christ-I am not lying; my conscience bears me witness in the Holy Spirit- that I have great sorrow and unceasing anguish in my heart. For I could wish that I myself were accursed and cut off from Christ for the sake of my brothers, my kinsmen according to the flesh. They are Israelites, and to them belong the adoption, the glory, the covenants, the giving of the law, the worship, and the promises.

To them belong the patriarchs, and from their race, according to the flesh, is the Christ who is God over all, blessed forever. Amen. But it is not as though the Word of God has failed. For not all who are descended from Israel belong to Israel, and not all are children of Abraham because they are his offspring, but "Through Isaac shall your offspring be named." This means that it is not the children of the flesh who are the children of God, but the offspring. For this is what the promise said: "About this time next year I will return, and Sarah shall have a son." And not only so, but also Rebekah had conceived children by one man, our forefather Isaac, though they were not yet born and had done nothing either good or bad-in order that God's purpose of election might continue, not because of works but because of him who calls-she was told, "The older will serve the younger." As it is written, "Jacob I loved, but Esau I hated." What shall we say then? Is there injustice on God's part? By no means! For he says to Moses, I will have mercy on whom I have mercy, and I will have compassion on whom I have compassion." So then it depends not on human will or exertion, but on God, who has mercy. For the Scripture says to Pharaoh, "For this very purpose I have raised you up, that I might show my power in you, and that my name might be proclaimed in all the earth." So then he has mercy on whomever he wills, and he hardens whomever he wills. You will say to me then, "Why then does he still find fault?" For who can resist his will?" But who are you, O man, to answer back to God? Will what is molded say to its molder, "Why have you made me like this?" Has the potter no right over the clay, to make out of the same lump one vessel for honorable use and another for dishonorable use? What if God, desiring to show his wrath and to make known his power, has endured with much patience vessels of wrath prepared for destruction, in order to make known the riches of his glory for vessels of mercy, which he has prepared beforehand for glory-even us whom he has called, not from the Jews only but also from the Gentiles? As indeed he says in Hosea, "Those who were not my people I will call 'my people', and her who was not beloved I will call 'beloved'." And in the very place where it was said to them 'You are not my people,' there they will be called sons of the living God." And Isaiah cries out concerning Israel: "Though the number of the sons of Israel be as the sand of the sea, only a remnant of them will be saved, for the Lord will carry out his sentence upon the earth fully and without delay." And as Isaiah has predicted, "If the Lord of hosts had not left us offspring, we would have become like Sodom and become like Gomorrah." What shall we say, then? That Gentiles who did not pursue righteousness have attained it, that is, a righteousness that is by faith; but that Israel who pursued a law that would lead to righteousness did not succeed in reaching that law. Why? Because they did not pursue it by faith, but as if it were based on works. They have stumbled over the stumbling stone, as it is written, "Behold, I am laying in Zion a stone of stumbling, and a rock of offense; and whoever believes in him will not be put to shame."

God's Sovereignty

In this passage of Scripture, we find a nugget of truth that shatters our human perception. You are probably reading this and saying that is not fair. Why does God have to be so sovereign? Why do things not work out the way I plan them. The reason is, "You are not your own!" That's right! You belong to God and when you make the decision to become a follower of Jesus Christ, you are just as the Word of God says "a follower." And you thought that you were in control! You had it all figured out huh? I will just pray, go to church, read my Bible, and then ZOOM, I will be in Heaven before you know it! Listen friend, God exist by Himself. That is what Sovereign means. He is all sufficient, All Powerful, and All Knowing! He is in control of your life. You might have many plans in your heart and many ways or places you would like to go but God will say NO. That is not My plan or that is not the way I want to work in your life. So the first thing you must understand about God is that "HE IS THE SOVEREIGN LORD!"

Mercy

The next thing is that He is merciful. He loves you like nobody else has or will love you. He cut-off Israel because of their disobedience and has grafted you in. He has called you His beloved and wants to go deeper with you. But He operates by mercy. I love the Word of God and the portion of Romans 9 that says it does not depend on human will or exertion, but on God, who has mercy. Praise God that it does not depend on me. Listen, God's plan for your life depends on His mercy. He has chosen to place this book in front of you for a purpose. It is the gospel of Jesus Christ! It is not for my gain, but for His. He has called you to preach the gospel! That's right! Why me? Because that is His will for everyone who calls Jesus Christ Lord. His mercy will be all over your life as you chose to be a vessel of mercy. And don't you think that you cannot be cut off as well. If God can cut-off Israel, He can cut-off you. So fear the Lord and know that God is merciful. One day He will graft a remnant of Israel back in, but He is waiting for you to be His grafting agent.

Faith

I have read many books and articles on faith, but nothing touches the Word of God. You see, the Bible says in Romans 10:17 that "Faith comes from hearing and hearing the Word of Christ." Israel was trying to form their own faith and that is why they were cut-off. They were good people because they did this or that. But God is not pleased with your fleshly attempts. He wants your "FAITH." Anything that is not from faith is sin. HUH? That is what the Word of God says. And this faith comes from hearing Jesus Christ speak His powerful Word into your life through the Holy Spirit. So stop trying to live a life for Christ that is based on your works. If you let the anointing of God flow through your life, your fruit will shine forth. You will not need the next greatest Christian leader to say "Hey brother you are a Christian!" No, the anointing of Christ will speak for you. I am amazed at the people I meet and they tell me that the Glory of God is all over me. I do not attempt to drum this up or say some special prayer or sing some special song. I just commune with the Lord and His Glory is seen upon me. That is the secret to living an obedient Christian life. Communion with Christ! O' the depths of His love, the riches of His presence. It is like warm heat on a cold day. His presence will make you whole.

So what about your life? Do you feel His presence? Are you submitting to His Sovereign plan, mercy, and faith? No matter what you are doing right now, stop and begin to worship the Lord. Spend 45 minutes with Him. Jared that is too long. Well, you spend 8-10 hours sleeping and you cannot spend 45 minutes with God. What's wrong with you! Well, I'm too busy Pastor Jared! Then when you get to Heaven you can explain that to God. But I know that He will not be pleased with your laziness. So hear His tender voice today saying "Come away 'My Beloved, Come away with me now, Come away 'My Beloved' Come away.

Chapter 7
Real Christianity

In the beginning of this book, I talked to you about some very precious things that God has done in my life. In this last chapter, I will be laying a foundation for all people to follow if they want to walk with Christ. This foundation consist of new birth, baptism in water, commitment to Christ, baptism in the Holy Spirit, commitment to the Word of God, and a public commitment to Christ.

New Birth

Hebrews 4:12-13 says "For the Word of God is living and active, sharper than any two-edged sword, piercing to the division of soul and spirit, of joints and marrow, and discerning the thoughts and intentions of the heart. And no creature is hidden from his sight, but all are naked and exposed to the eyes of him to whom we must give account.

This portion of God's Word tells us the power of the Word of God. It is to bring a new birth experience by continuing to lead those who read it to Jesus Christ. This new birth happens when one confesses sin to Jesus Christ, turns from sin, and then asks that the Lord Jesus Christ would live in them.

Furthermore, after this individual becomes born-again, he or she is changed into a new person. A man by the name of Nicodemus asked Jesus "Can a man pass through his mother's womb a second time?" And that may by some of the questions associated with being born-again. But listen friend, this new life means that all of your past is gone, so that all of His future can be fulfilled in your life. You are given a new life to live. This life is found in the Word of God and by keeping in step with the Spirit. It is important to understand that unless you are given this new life, then you are not an authentic follow of Jesus Christ.

Baptism in Water

Many people and churches fall short on this truth. They see it abused by other denominations or religions and say "Well, we will not major in this area!" I want to speak to you! Baptism is a foundation of the Christian faith.

In the days of Jesus Christ, his ministry was accompanied by repentance and baptism. Many other followers of Christ and leaders were baptized.

So in this new life in Christ, Baptism is a foundational truth that must accompany your salvation experience. If this is not followed, then you are disobeying the Word of God. I charge you this day to follow your repentance with Baptism in water.

Commitment to Christ

The next truth that I want to speak into your life is that you must have a solid commitment to Christ. He has to be LORD of LORDS and KING of KINGS in every area of your life. You must anchor yourself in

Him in order to be an effective Christian.

If you think of a boat, it has a number of things that it uses to catch a fish. But if it has no anchor than the waves will blow the ship away from the fish. You see, the fish is the fisherman's harvest. If he does not catch any, he does not eat. It is the same with your life in Christ. Jesus Christ is the anchor of your salvation. If you do not remain committed to Him than your desired harvest (which is your salvation) will be swept away by the waves of this world! "But Pastor Jared, I do not believe that I can lose my salvation because I did not work to achieve it, it was by grace." Yes, it was by grace. But you see the source of grace is Jesus Christ. If you cut yourself off from Christ by not being committed to Him then you lose your new life and your initial commitment was probably not sincere at all.

Baptism in the Holy Spirit

Another great foundation that was laid in the

Word of God was the baptism in the Holy Spirit. Although this is probably one of the most attacked foundations in the Word of God, we must be baptized in the Holy Spirit if we want to be effective. So let's talk about three things concerning the baptism in the Spirit. They are the indwelling of the person & power of the Holy Spirit, tongues, and signs following.

I would like to give you an illustration that may shed some light on this whole matter. Think of a costume. In itself, the costume is useless. It can only be used when someone is inside it. We put them on for party occasions, school dances, and possibly the fourth of July. After we are done, we take them off and get back to our regular lives.

The Holy Spirit works in a similar way. He fills the believer not during salvation, but after salvation and only when a believer desires Him. He steps into your body and lives inside of you. He has a purpose for your life to fulfill and He wants to do this through your body. He is very different than you, but His plans are always successful.

Furthermore, while I used this illustration to help give you some understanding of the baptism in the Spirit, one thing that I do want you to understand is that He is not a costume. He is God and once He is in, He stays. The only way that you can get Him to leave is if you completely turn away from Christ. So then, the Holy Spirit should be permanently present in the life of every believer.

The evidence of tongues is the next sign that a believer is filled with the Holy Spirit. "Hold on Pastor Jared, "You are wrong!" No! The Word of God is right! The Bible says that one of the signs of the baptism in the Holy Spirit is speaking in tongues. When the believers in the New Testament were filled with the Holy Spirit, they all spoke in tongues. So then, we can set a standard of truth that tongues is a sign that one is filled with the Holy Spirit and if you did not speak in tongues then you are not filled. Many people disagree with this, but it is truth. As a believer you have a choice to either let someone else's opinion about God's Word be your foundation or you can let God's Word be your foundation.

The last thing about the Baptism in the Holy Spirit is that there will be signs following. I cannot give you a complete description of what those signs will be because the Holy Spirit is far greater than my imagination. But some of the Biblical signs are Christians living a life that honors Christ (Fruits of the Spirit), people being saved as they come in contact with the gospel message, baptizing people in water, physical healing, deliverance from demons, praying in tongues, prophecy, and other gifts of the Spirit. While these are some of them, I do not want to limit the Holy Spirit by saying that this is the only way that He will work in your life. He can do exceedingly abundantly above all that you can hope or imagine. So let Him fill your life with this great foundation so that you can be an effective follower of Christ.

Word of God

Here is where rubber meets the road. If you disagreed with anything that I said previously in this chapter, this is why! The Word of God is the greatest foundation for our lives. It is the map, compass, and tour guide. I love going on vacation knowing that I will reach my final destination. But if I cannot get there successfully, then what is the point of going. That is one of the reasons God has given us the Bible. So that we can arrive at the final destination with no confusion or misunderstanding of how we got there. He charts the course, sets the sails, and then says "Come follow Me!" What an adventure! What an exciting life! I am so glad that I chose to follow the map of God's Word in my life. For it has been a great joy to my heart and life.

In your life, always read the Bible. Do not let anything else change your worldview. Be biblically minded in everything that you do and I promise that God will be with you all of the way.

Public Commitment to Christ

The last thing that I want to talk about is a public commitment to Christ. This commitment is based on you sharing your faith & being connected to a local body of believers. We call this church. Many believe that going to church is not a foundational truth since the church is not a building. But they fail to miss the body of Christ inside the building. Hey, I am a Pastor and I am telling you that we don't thrive on the whole building thing either. Trust me; to have a building it takes lots of money. If we could have church outside all the time, we would. But we have the weather, need places to sit, and need rooms to hold small discipleship groups.

Furthermore, we do this for you. Believers give 10% of their earnings and some even more in order to give you a place to connect with other believers. This allows you to worship God, hear the Word of God preached, and build authentic Christian friendships. Plus it is the heart of God. The Bible says that we are the body of Christ. That means when you believe in Jesus you are plugged into the local church by faith. Now all that you have to do is go there. I know that it may seem kind of intimidating sometimes, but once your there you will build friendships that will last a lifetime. So I challenge you to be a total Christian and don't sell yourself short of anything less.

Final Words

I hope that you have enjoyed this journey of faith through "He Took My Place." This book was written for your own benefit. So if nothing is applied than nothing will be gained. But I can promise you that if you apply the biblical principles in this book that God will bless your life in many ways. My prayer for you is that Christ will change your life, bring you to His Word, and use you to furthermore His body, "The Church."

LaVergne, TN USA
07 April 2010
178469LV00004B/9/P